WHAT IS A
Legend?

ROBYN HARDYMAN

Britannica®
Educational Publishing

IN ASSOCIATION WITH

ROSEN
EDUCATIONAL SERVICES

Published in 2014 by Britannica Educational Publishing (a trademark of Encyclopædia Britannica, Inc.) in association with The Rosen Publishing Group, Inc.
29 East 21st Street, New York, NY 10010

Distributed exclusively by Rosen Publishing.
To see additional Britannica Educational Publishing titles, go to rosenpublishing.com

First Edition

Britannica Educational Publishing
J.E. Luebering: Director, Core Reference Group
Anthony L. Green: Editor, Compton's by Britannica

Rosen Publishing
Hope Lourie Killcoyne: Executive Editor
Nelson Sá: Art Director

Library of Congress Cataloging-in-Publication Data

Hardyman, Robyn.
What is a Legend? / Robyn Hardyman. — First Edition.
    pages cm. — (The Britannica Common Core Library)
 Includes bibliographical references and index.
 ISBN 978-1-62275-205-8 (library binding) — ISBN 978-1-62275-208-9 (pbk.) — ISBN 978-1-62275-209-6 (6-pack)
 1. Legends—Juvenile literature. I. Title.
 GR78.H37 2014
 398.2—dc23
                                                                                                 2013022571

Manufactured in the United States of America.

Photo credits
Cover: Shutterstock: Fer Gregory r, Nejron Photo l. Inside: Dreamstime: Aliencat 17, Andreyuu 18, Jfeinstein 23, Konstantin32 4, Littlemacproductions 16, Lvnel 21, Marafona738 26–27, Pancaketom 8, Philcold 11, Rabbit75 22, Rcpsi 25, Russelllinton 24, Troutlake3339 12–13; Flickr: Robert Blackie 19; Shutterstock: Sushko Anastasia 9, Catmando 6, Ensiferum 28–29, Fer Gregory 1r, Igor Kovalchuk 7, Nejron Photo 1l, 14–15, Wavebreakmedia 5.

CONTENTS

What Is a Legend?

Long ago, people told stories that were based on history, but were not completely true. They are called legends. Legends tell of a time, place, or person as though the events actually took place. Robin Hood is an example of a legend.

Robin Hood is based on a man named Robin of Loxley, who lived in England in the 1200s.

In real life, Robin of Loxley was probably in trouble with the law. In legend, he became Robin Hood, a man who took money from the rich to help the poor.

Legends were first told aloud and passed down through many generations. This meant that many versions of the same story were told. Eventually, legends were written down.

Generations are groups of people born at around the same time.

The legends we read in books today were first told long ago.

Why Are Legends Told?

People have always told stories about the past. They told legends to each generation to teach them about their culture. Today, legends teach us something about the culture of people in the past.

Many Native American legends include horses and eagles because they were important to Native American culture.

The setting of each legend is important because it tells people about the place they come from. For example, the Inuit legend of Tikta'liktak is about a man's journey across the ice. He faces many dangers on the way, such as polar bears. The Inuit lived in cold, icy places such as Alaska, where polar bears were a terrible threat. It was important for people in the past to understand the dangers around them, and know how to deal with them.

A **threat** is something that is so dangerous it could cause harm.

Themes in Legends

There are legends from different parts of the world. They all tell stories of people and their actions. There are many legends about kings and **heroes** who shaped nations.

There are also legends about places that are important to a group of people. They explain how the world around them was created.

Devils Tower

Heroes are people who do very brave or wonderful things.

8

The legend of Devils Tower in Wyoming was told by Native Americans. For them, this mountain is sacred. In the legend, a bear chased some children onto a low rock. The rock grew and grew. It became a mountain, lifting the children out of the bear's reach. The angry bear scraped its claws on the rock, leaving marks on the mountain.

Bears were a common danger for Native Americans.

Legends Retold

Now that we know what legends are and why they are told, let's read and **compare** some wonderful legends from around the world.

The Legend of King Arthur

This legend comes from Britain.

Long ago, King Uther Pendragon lived in Britain. When he died, people fought about who should be king. A magician named Merlin set a sword in a stone. Merlin said whoever pulled the sword from the stone would be king. Only King Uther's son, Arthur, could pull the sword from the stone.

> **Compare** means to look at two or more things to see how alike or different they are.

Arthur became king and led his people in battle against invaders from Europe. Arthur and his knights carried out acts of great bravery.

The Lady of the Lake gave Arthur a magical sword, called Excalibur. When Arthur died, the sword was returned to the Lady of the Lake.

King Arthur's sword, Excalibur, was believed to have magical powers.

The Legend of Hiawatha

The Native Americans tell the legend of Hiawatha.

Hiawatha was a Native American chief. He was tired of the fighting between the five nations that lived in his area. The Great Peacemaker told Hiawatha that the way to bring peace was to join the five nations into one nation.

The name of Hiawatha's daughter, Minnehaha, means "running water."

The leader of one of the five nations, the Onondagas, did not want to form one nation. He sent a white bird to take Hiawatha's daughter, Minnehaha, and kill her. Even after Minnehaha's death, Hiawatha worked with the five nations. He told them that by uniting they could beat their enemies. They agreed to form the Iroquois **Confederacy**. Hiawatha then said farewell, telling the tribes to live wisely.

A **confederacy** is a group of states or peoples who agree to join together.

13

Let's Compare

The legends of Arthur and Hiawatha are about wise and powerful leaders. Both Arthur and Hiawatha become leaders when their lands are in danger from invaders. They help them through trouble.

Arthur probably did exist, in the 500s, when fierce fighters called the Anglo-Saxons invaded Britain. The legend of Arthur began in 1133, when a man named Geoffrey of Monmouth wrote down the stories about Arthur's life.

Hiawatha was also a real person. He lived in the 1500s in the region that was to become New York state. At that time, the five Native American nations were being attacked from the north. Hiawatha worked to unite them, creating the Iroquois Confederacy. The magical detail of his story, such as the great white bird that takes Minnehaha, was important in Native American culture.

Stories about Arthur are set in medieval times.

The Legend of Atlantis
This legend comes from ancient Greece.

When the gods of ancient Greece divided up the land, Poseidon, god of the sea, was given the island of Atlantis. The island lay in the Atlantic Ocean.

Poseidon made his son, Atlas, the king of Atlantis and of the ocean. Poseidon carved the island's main mountain into a palace. The palace became a beautiful, rich city.

Poseidon gave the large island of Atlantis to his son.

Some people believe Atlantis lies undiscovered beneath the ocean. This painting shows how the ruined city beneath the ocean might look.

One day, there was a terrible earthquake. It caused a huge wave in the ocean that swallowed Atlantis. The beautiful city vanished, lost beneath the waves forever.

STORYTELLERS

The only account of the story of Atlantis is by a Greek thinker named Plato, who lived about 2,300 years ago.

The Legend of El Dorado

This legend comes from the Muisca tribe, who lived in Colombia, in South America.

El Dorado was the chief, or Zipa, of the Muisca tribe. His name means "the gilded one." The Muisca worshipped a goddess with offerings of gold. In an important ceremony, the Zipa covered himself in gold dust. He put gold objects onto a raft, and climbed onto it. The raft was pushed out onto the holy lake, Lake Guatavita. As people watched, the chief offered the gold dust on his body to the goddess by diving into the lake.

When Spanish invaders arrived in South America in the 1500s, they heard rumors of the Muisca's gold. They believed that Lake Guatavita was rich with gold, so they drained the lake. They found little gold, and decided the kingdom of El Dorado must be somewhere else. The Spanish then set off to find it.

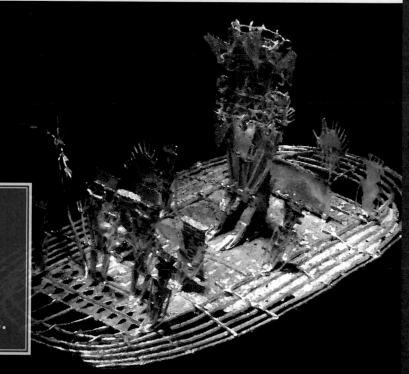

This model shows the Zipa floating out onto Lake Guatavita on a raft loaded with golden offerings for the goddess.

Let's Compare

The legends of Atlantis and El Dorado are about **wealthy** places. Atlantis was an island where the people were wealthy. El Dorado came to mean city of gold, with endless wealth.

Atlantis probably never existed. It is a story about a perfect place that makes people feel happy when they think about it. However, the story could be based on a real event. Long ago, a volcano erupted on the island of Thera. This caused a huge wave that could have covered another island, or Thera itself could have been Atlantis and was covered by the wave.

Wealthy means to have a lot of money.

El Dorado was originally a person, not a place. The Spanish heard of his golden offerings, and the legend spread. In the story, El Dorado became a city made of gold. For years, Europeans searched for El Dorado but no one ever found the legendary city.

A hunger for gold made the legend of El Dorado grow among Europeans.

Alligators in New York

One famous modern legend is about the city of New York.

Nearly 100 years ago, so the story goes, some New Yorkers went to Florida on vacation. They visited the alligators there, bringing home baby alligators for their children to keep as pets. When the alligators grew too big, the parents flushed them down the toilet.

Modern legends can grow from small events. As they are told, the legends spread as if the stories are true.

*Some of these alligators are said to have survived in the **sewers**. They had babies. Then, their babies had babies. Now some people believe that there are lots of fierce alligators in the sewers. Because they never see daylight, the alligators are white instead of brown. From time to time, the legend has it, a poor sewer worker catches sight of one of these terrible creatures!*

Sewers are large underground pipes that transport waste from people's toilets.

This public sculpture is based on the alligators in New York legend!

The Legend of Big Foot

This is an American legend.

*Big Foot, or **Sasquatch**, is a large, hairy creature, a little like an ape. It walks upright on two legs. Most scientists consider Big Foot to be folklore or misidentification. However, some people think it lives in the forests of the northwestern United States. People have also reported seeing it in other parts of the country, and in Canada. They say Big Foot comes out mostly at night.*

BIG FOOT XING

DUE TO SIGHTINGS IN THE AREA OF A CREATURE RESEMBLING "BIG FOOT" THIS SIGN HAS BEEN POSTED FOR YOUR SAFETY

Could Big Foot be prowling the country? Some people believe so!

Reports say that Big Foot is 6 to 10 feet (1.8 to 3 m) tall. It has thick legs and is covered in reddish brown hair. People who think they saw Big Foot say they also smelled something terrible when they saw the beast. Footprints, up to 2 feet (60 cm) long were also found. People say Big Foot is very strong and can run fast. The beast has been heard whistling, roaring, and even screaming.

Sasquatch comes from the word "sasqets." The word was used by the original people of southeastern Canada and means "wild man."

Let's Compare

The legend of the alligators in the sewers and Big Foot are about something scary. Sometimes, people like to be a little scared because it can be exciting. People also like to believe the impossible, or unlikely.

Just like ghost stories or spooky movies, scary modern legends can be exciting.

Alligators could not survive in the sewers of New York. It is too cold for them to live there. The sewage would also poison them. The legend cannot be true. There are many legends about "wild men" such as Big Foot from cultures all around the world. They have been told for hundreds of years to entertain children and to excite them.

These modern legends tell us something about our world and our beliefs. They show what we are afraid of, or what we think is funny.

Write Your Own Legend

Are you ready to write your own legend? Here are some simple steps to help you start:

1. Historic or modern? Decide whether your legend will be set in the past or be a modern legend based on life today.

2. Pick your subject: If you are writing about the past, choose a time or a person in history that interests you. Or you could write about an interesting feature in the landscape near where you live, and describe how it came to be the way it is today.

3. **Think of a plot:** Your legend could be about someone's bravery or remarkable achievement.

4. **Find your characters**: Along with your hero, choose other characters, too. They can also include animals.

5. **Sketch out your legend:** Make a "map" of the story, showing the start, middle, and end.

6. **Write and rewrite!** Write your legend, then read it through and change anything you do not like.

Finished? Read your legend to a friend or a family member. E-mail it to your teacher, your family, and friends. You could post it onto your family's website or blog.

Legends are often about heroes who face enormous challenges, but who win in the end.

brave Feeling or showing no fear.

characters The people or animals in a legend.

chief The leader of a group of people.

culture The customs and traditions of a group of people.

earthquake A violent movement of part of Earth's surface.

erupted Exploded.

gilded Golden.

history Things that happened in the past.

Inuit A member of a group of people who live in the Arctic.

invaders Warlike people who try to take over a country or region.

knights Medieval soldiers.

magician A person who can perform magic tricks.

medieval Relating to the Middle Ages—the period in European history from about 500 to 1500.

misidentification When something is identified incorrectly.

plot Events that happen in a story.

raft A vessel similar to a boat, which floats on water.

rumors Stories, which are often a mixture of truth and untruth, that are told or spread by people.

sacred Holy.

setting Where a story takes place.

survived Continued to live.

themes Ideas found in stories.

uniting Joining together.

vanished Disappeared.

volcano A mountain that erupts with hot rocks and ash, which pour out of the top of the volcano and cover the land around it.

Books

dePaola Tomie. *Tomie dePaola's Big Book of Favorite Legends.* New York, NY: Putnam Juvenile, 2007.

Lancelyn Green, Roger. *The Adventures of Robin Hood* (Puffin Classics). New York, NY: Puffin Books, 2010.

Milbourne, Anna, Heather Amery, and Gillian Doherty. *The Usborne Book of Myths and Legends*. Tulsa, OK: Usborne, 2007.

Schoolcraft, Henry R. *The Enchanted Moccasins and Other Native American Legends* (Dover Children's Classics). Mineola, NY: Dover Publications, 2007.

Stone, Janet. *How to Tell a Legend*. New York, NY: Crabtree Publishing Company, 2011.

Websites

Due to the changing nature of Internet links, Rosen Publishing has developed an online list of Websites related to the subject of this book. This site is updated regularly. Please use this link to access the list:

http://www.rosenlinks.com/corel/leg

INDEX